THE UNICORN

MEDITATIONS ON THE LOVE OF GOD

HARRY GALBRAITH MILLER

SLG Press
Convent of the Incarnation
Fairacres Oxford

ISBN 0 7283 0124 5

ISSN 0307-1405

ACKNOWLEDGEMENTS

The tapestry shown on the cover is *The Hunt of the Unicorn*: VII: The Unicorn in Captivity, wool and silk with metal threads. From the Chateau of Verteuil. The Metropolitan Museum of Art, The Cloisters Collection, New York, Gift of John D. Rockefeller, Jr., 1937.

The tapestry shown on page vi is *La Dame à la Licorne*: V (detail): Musée de Cluny, Paris, cliché des Musées Nationaux.

We are grateful for permission to use both illustrations.

TO
THE DEAR MEMORY OF
MY MOTHER
SERVANT AND FRIEND OF
JESUS CHRIST
TO WHOM BE ALL PRAISE AND GLORY.

Argentum et aurum non est mihi,
quod autem habeo, hoc tibi do.
Acts 3: 6

PREFACE

These meditations or studies, call them what you like, started life as sermons preached in the Parish Church on Iona, where the memory of St Columba is still fragrant. They however bear little resemblance in their present form to the originals. I have to confess with Bunyan that, when I first began to meddle with this matter, 'I felt myself . . . so empty, spiritless, and barren, that I thought I should not have been able to speak among them so much as five words of truth with life and evidence.' However, 'methought the more I cast mine eye upon the whole discourse, the more I saw lie in it. Wherefore setting myself to a more narrow search, through prayer to God, what first with doing, and then with undoing, and after that with doing again, I thus did finish it.' I do not pretend that these little essays bear any comparison with Bunyan's *Holy City*, but when first delivered they were of interest to the few who heard them, and, it may be, they may interest others.

I must particularly thank the Sisters of the SLG Press for showing me the significance of the Unicorn Tapestries at the Cloisters in New York. I had known about them, but they had made very little impact on me until I saw them through their eyes. I am grateful to them.

Harry Galbraith Miller
Port Bannatyne 1989

v

La Dame à la Licorne, Musée de Cluny, cliché des Musées Nationaux (See p. 37).

CHRISTMAS DAY

Will the unicorn be willing to serve thee, or abide by thy crib? *(Job 39: 9)*

IN the summer of 1982 I found myself pondering the deep meaning of the legend of the unicorn—which everyone in our clever modern world knows to be a fabulous creature that never was in the ark with Noah, even though Aristotle and Pliny may have believed firmly in its existence. Then in October, with thoughts of the unicorn still in mind, I was in Paris and there discovered the wonderful fifteenth century tapestries of the Lady with the Unicorn: *La Dame à la Licorne*. I shall return to these tapestries more particularly later; at the moment it is sufficient to say that I stood entranced, drinking in their glory and beauty for over two hours. Here I note only two things.

The first is this. My friends (or at least the more gullible) were impressed by the fact that I knew about these tapestries.

> *And still they gazed, and still the wonder grew,*
> *That one small head could carry all he knew.* [1]

But the significant fact was that I had never heard of *La Dame à la Licorne* in my life. I only turned into the Musée de Cluny because it was beginning to rain and I had no umbrella. To encounter so unexpectedly the unicorn about which I had been thinking all summer, seemed to me, and still seems, to be something more than a coincidence. My thoughts were being forced in this direction whether I liked it or not.

The other point is this. Scholars have known for centuries that whatever strange and terrible beast was meant by the Hebrew word *Re'em*, it was certainly not the unicorn. Jerome in the fourth century translated it as *Rhinoceros*, which is as good a guess as any, while modern scholars seem to prefer to translate it as *Wild Ox*. The very considerable scholars who prepared the King James version in 1611 chose, however, to go back to the unicorn, which was the translation of the Septuagint. I found myself wondering why. Perhaps there was a subtle compliment to the king. When James VI added England to his crown, he replaced one of the lions, which

1

were supporters of the English royal arms, by the Scottish unicorn. But there is far more to it than that. There was almost certainly a reference to the meaning of the unicorn in Christian symbolism. It had, we are told, a body like a horse, a head like a goat, a tail like a lion, and on its forehead one tremendous and sharp twisted horn. That is not important here. What is important is that it was fierce and untamable, and so fleet of foot that no hunter could catch it. Yet there was a way in which it could be trapped. If it saw a pure young virgin, it at once ran towards her and lay down at her feet, gentle and tame. Then it could be captured easily and killed. Therefore the unicorn became one of the symbols for our Saviour, who in his eternal Godhead is terrible in majesty and glory, untamable and unconquerable, but who entered into a pure virgin, and held by the unbreakable chains of his own love, died for love, even as he had come to us in love.

Will the unicorn be willing to serve thee, or abide by thy crib? The message of Christmas is surely just this, that the Creator of the world has become the Servant of the world, and the Ruler and Lord of all things has condescended to the crib of Bethlehem. It is the message of the unimaginable, almost unbelievable, love of God who made himself of no reputation, and took upon him the form of a servant and humbled himself, and all for love. There is so little of it in the world. Emotionalism and sentimentality we have in plenty, but the love that suffers long and is kind, the love that has in it no envy, the love that seeketh not its own and is not easily provoked, the love that bears all things, believes all things, hopes all things and endures all things, the love that never fails (cf. I Cor. 13), that is something else and is rare enough. We live in a world where people are exploited for gain, and that is not the way of love. It is a world where the strong are selfish and the weak envious and bitter, and that is not the way of love. It is a world in which millions are hungry, and homeless, and without work, a world where people no longer feel that they belong or are needed, and where consequently they are desperately lonely, and that is not the way of love. It is world in which marriages break down irretrievably at the first strain that is put upon them, where children are at odds with their parents, and parents are tactless, and neither is prepared to be forbearing and try to understand the other, and that is not the way of love. Yet people are hungry for the warmth and glory of love, and that is what the message of Christmas is about.

I had thought to write the 'security of love' rather than 'the glory of love', but the word 'security' is not an appropriate word to use here, for there is, in fact, nothing more terrifying than love. It leaves you naked and without defence, and so we wrap the whole thing up in emotionalism and make-believe, and if we are not careful Christmas becomes only another of man's games of 'let's pretend'. Yet the battle in the world is real enough. The forces of aggression and the forces of love are locked in a mortal conflict. The lion and the unicorn are fighting for the crown. It is not pretty, and the one thing that we must surely not do is to wrap the whole thing up in conventional Christmas decorations, and push the stern realities of this tragic world out of sight for a little. It will not do simply to give the lion and the unicorn plum cake and drum them both out of town. The traditional Christmas story is lovely beyond words, and every year we are held by the magic of the new born baby lying in the crib watched by his gentle and holy mother. But it you want to know what Christmas is really about, I will direct you to another passage of scripture:

> Jesus knew that his hour was come, and though he knew that his Father had given all things into his hands, and that he had come forth from God and was soon to return to God, he rose from the table in the middle of supper, rolled up his sleeves and took a towel and tied it round him, and washed his disciples' feet.

Then he explained what it was that he had done:

> I am your Lord and Master, and I have washed your feet: you also ought to wash one another's feet. For I have given you an example, that you should do as I have done to you. (cf. John 13:1–17)

The unicorn was willing to serve us, and to abide by our crib. That is to say, the example we are called to follow is the example of him who was among us as one that serves, and who serves not from a superior place from which with infinite condescension he might play the gracious benefactor. He went lower than the humblest: he was born in a stable: he had no advantage over the poorest, the economically weakest, the ·politically most dispossessed. In one thing only had he the advantage. No one could love as he loved. As Professor Arthur Curtis wrote, 'He has out-listened, and out-imagined and out-loved all.'[2]

When the unicorn ran to the virgin he did not escape from danger into security. Because of his love for her he was content to be vulnerable. So when Christ was born in Bethlehem he was not escaping from the harsh realities of the world, but entering them—with a love that refused to defend itself. He began by being homeless: he was soon to be, with his parents, a political refugee: all his life he was to be at risk—and all for love. He still calls for followers, and those who follow will not find Christmas a warm retreat from the menace of life. An old Scottish minister is alleged to have preached a sermon on the text, 'Follow thou me', which he divided under four heads. 'First,' he said, 'there are followers ahint; secondly, there are followers afore; thirdly, there are followers cheekie for chow, and sidie by sidie; and last of a' there are followers that stand stane-still.' It was extraordinarily astute. We all know the followers who stand still, though it is perhaps worth reminding ourselves that if we have time to observe them, it is probably because we are standing still ourselves. There is no need to digress here to those who would follow cheek by jowl, side by side with the Master, with their hand in his oxter, as though they were his equals and could suffer like him or love like him. Nor need we speak of those who follow in front, who know better than Christ where they ought to be going, and have such confidence in themselves that they would choose the path and expect him to follow. John says sarcastically of them that they run ahead and outrun the Gospel of Christ (II John: 9 NEB). The Master will not follow meekly behind even the most enthusiastic of such followers, who know better than he what has to be done and how it should be done, and who have little or nothing of his infinite patience. The only followers who matter are those who follow humbly in their Master's footsteps, go where he leads and live in the spirit of love in which he lived.

'Will the unicorn be willing to serve thee, or abide by thy crib?' That is no longer the question. He has done so, and still does. The question now is: will his followers be willing to serve him, and will they abide by his crib? Now there must be no mistake here. It is *followers* that Christ calls for. As Kierkegaard pointed out, 'He never says anything about wanting admirers, admiring worshippers, adherents.'[3] And he certainly does not call for imitators, even though, we are told, imitation may be the sincerest form of flattery. Imitation is the lowest form of art, even of the art of living, because there is in it nothing creative, and those who follow the Creative Word of God, who never makes two souls alike and who is constantly bringing forth what is new, must be prepared to live lives that are distinctively their own, lives that add something new to the world, something that to all eternity would have been lacking from the hymn of praise that creation offers to God if they had never lived. It is no simple unison that the creation sings, but an unimaginable harmony in which no two notes are the same, and which yet is no discord but a thing of utter beauty. So the followers of Christ do not imitate him, trying to copy his actions literally and meticulously. There can be no replica of Christ for he is unique, the Son of Man who is Son of God. When we say of anyone that he is Christlike, we mean rather that we recognize in him the same spirit of self-forgetting and self-denying love that is in the life of our Lord. He has in him the mind of Christ, who though he was in the form of God took the form of a servant. He abides by the crib of the Saviour, and having received of his Spirit lives a life of creative love.

It is this light of love that at Christmas came into the darkness of human selfishness. It is this love, so totally incapable of counting the cost to itself, that we celebrate. It is no wonder that it set the angels singing. But it has more admirers on earth than followers. It is too daunting. It began among the smells and draughts of a stable, with an almost indecent lack of privacy. It must still be lived in the bitterness of the world, where men fight and struggle, and hate and love, bless and curse. It is lived from the manger, and can only be lived from there. It is credibly reported that there was once a notice on a church door which read, 'This is the gate of heaven.' Underneath was another notice, 'Please keep this door shut to keep out the draughts.'

The door of Christmas is always open to the draughts of life, for it tells of him who came among us drawn by love to expose himself to risk, and held by love amid all life's sorrows, to give light to them that sit in darkness and to guide our feet into the way of peace.

GOOD FRIDAY

*Save me from the lion's mouth; for thou hast heard me
from the horns of the unicorns. (Ps. 22:21)*

THIS deeply disturbing, indeed shattering psalm is for obvious reasons one
of those appointed in all churches for Good Friday. No Christian can read
it without being brought into that holy place where our Lord offered himself for the sins of the whole world, and was abandoned to death amid the
jeers and taunts of those whom he loved.

My God, my God, why hast thou forsaken me? why art thou so far
from helping me? . . . I am . . . despised of the people. All they that see
me laugh me to scorn: they shoot out the lip, they shake the head,
saying, He trusted in the Lord that he would deliver him: let him
deliver him, seeing he delighted in him . . . Thou hast brought me into
the dust of death. For dogs have compassed me: the assembly of the
wicked have inclosed me: they pierced my hands and my feet. They
part my garments among them, and cast lots upon my vesture. But be
not thou far from me, O Lord . . . Save me from the lion's mouth.

Then suddenly, unbelievably, like a vivid flash of lightning bursting from
black and impenetrable clouds, the triumphant cry, 'Thou hast heard me
from the horns of the unicorns.' (cf. Ps. 22: 1–21 AV)

So unexpected is this sudden cry of victorious faith, so inexplicable in
face of the darkness and abandonment that have gone before it, that most
modern translations assume that the text cannot be correct, and amend it
to read as a further call for help: '(Save) my afflicted soul from the horns
of the unicorns.' Yet it seems to me that the Hebrew text should be left
undisturbed. The dividing line between despair and faith can be a mere
hair's breadth, and when the soul is at the very verge of the bottomless
abyss, it can in an instant be snatched into safety. There does not need to
be any long twilight separating darkness from dawn. The one can follow
the other instantaneously. This most of us know well enough, for when all
is going well with us and we have no fears and no anxieties, despair, or

6

near despair, can grip us in a swift and complete blackness with not even one star visible to guide us. Similarly, though it may not be so common in our experience, since we more often have to struggle slowly and most agonizingly up from darkness into the light of faith, yet it can happen and does happen that in a flash the darkness is past and the true light is shining round us. So here we may safely take the Bible as it speaks to us out of its own faith. Bitter cry follows bitter cry, expostulation follow expostulation. 'Why hast thou forsaken me? Save me from the lion's mouth'–and then, against all calculation, the shout of victory: 'Thou hast heard me–thou hast answered me, and that from the very horns of the unicorns.'

Here too fresh depths of meaning are opened to us if we retain the Authorized Version's translation, 'the horns of the unicorns'. We have already seen how this terrible creature, that could only be tamed by its love for a pure virgin, stood in earlier ages for a symbol of Christ, and nowhere more fittingly than here. As Paul says, all the fullness of the Godhead dwelt in him: the whole power of God was at his disposal, and yet he would not use it: he could not use it without being false to his whole being. He was held captive by love, and (this is where the truth is more amazing than the legend) it was not by the love of what was pure and beautiful, but by the love of what was soiled and betrayed and degraded. So absolute is this love that it leaves him committed up to the hilt. 'If it be possible, let this cup pass from me', Christ had prayed in the Garden of Gethsemane, but it was not possible except on terms that were for him impossible. Only by abandoning those whom he loved could he escape drinking the cup.

The chief priests and scribes and elders mocked Christ because, though he had saved others, he could not save himself. 'If he be the King of Israel,' they cried, 'let him now come down from the cross, and we will believe him' (Matt. 27:42). Of course they would have believed on those terms. That was the only kind of behaviour that they were capable of understanding. If Christ had shown his kingly power by scattering his enemies and delivering himself, they would certainly have believed, for that was the kind of leader they were longing and praying for. That was a sign they could have accepted and which would have convinced them. In a sense it is the only kind of behaviour that most of us think rational. But it was the one sign that Christ could not give. The unicorn could not tear itself away from the place to which its love had brought it. It was not possible. The priests, quoting this psalm, argued, 'He trusted in God: let him deliver him now if he will have him.' It was not, I think, just a sneer, though there was a sneer in it. They remembered, no doubt, that the psalm ended in the

7

triumphant vindication of the sufferer, and some spectacular deliverance would have been accepted by them, but all that was to be seen was abysmal failure, and such failure was too pitiful, the clear sign of the deluded impostor. It was not given to men to understand, till much later, that the truly abysmal failure would have been for Christ to have come down from the Cross. So Christ hung there, hour after hour, and in that lay his victory. God heard him from the horns of the unicorns. It is a highly strained interpretation of the psalm, but an utterly true reading of the events of the Cross, that God answered and delivered his Son by sustaining him in a love that would not save itself. Because he was not only truly God but was also truly man, our Lord cannot have had absolute knowledge that Good Friday would be followed by Easter. As he hung upon the Cross it must have seemed to him that God had rejected his life's work. All his obedience to the Father's will, as he understood it, had gone for nothing. His faith and trust had been misplaced. His love had been spurned. All his hopes and dreams were in ruins. But the last and the fiercest battle was still to be fought: the battle against bitterness and hatred—bitterness against God who had deceived and then deserted him; hatred of men who had rejected him with contempt. Had that battle been lost, all would have been lost: but it was not lost. Having loved his own which were in the world, he loved them to the uttermost. This was a love that bore it out even to the edge of doom—and far beyond. Having loved his Father in all his life, he loved him in the darkness of failure and rejection. Because of that love he was heard and delivered. He was not saved from the love that is utterly defenceless, but in and because of it he was saved. He was not saved from being mangled by the horns of the unicorns, but in the agony of crucifixion, when he was ferociously gored and trampled to death, his inmost being was preserved inviolate. He had himself said to his disciples, 'Fear not them which kill the body, but are not able to kill the soul' (Matt. 10:28), and now in the very centre of defeat he found himself held secure. Through failure he had come to victory.

The amazing transition from the torment and despair with which this psalm opens to the triumphant cry, 'Thou hast heard me from the horns of the unicorns', is not more amazing than the sudden transition from 'Eloi, Eloi, lama sabachthani,' to 'It is finished. Father, into thy hands I commend my spirit.' It is not necessarily a long journey from hell to heaven, because as the psalmist says, 'If I make my bed in hell, behold, thou art there' (Ps. 139:8). In as real a way Christ found God in hell as he hung upon the Cross, as he had found him on the Mount of Transfiguration.

8

On the Mount he had spoken with Moses and Elijah about the death he was to die at Jerusalem, and the watching disciples heard a voice saying, 'This is my beloved Son, in whom I am well pleased.' On the Cross our Saviour was indeed again transfigured, and few could have recognized in this broken figure, foul with dust and sweat, twisted with pain and disfigured with torture, the calm, regal Son of David to whom the crowds had shouted Hosanna only six days before, when he rode on an ass into Jerusalem. Yet it is certain, more certain than anything else in our faith, that he was still the Beloved Son in whom God was well pleased. Even when broken and mangled by the horns of the unicorns, he was still the Beloved Son. It was because he was the Beloved Son that he went the way of the Cross in faithful obedience.

If I were to be asked how I know, how I can be so sure, that this Jesus of Nazareth is indeed the Son of God, I do not think that I would point either to his miraculous powers over nature—his miracles—or to his extraordinary psychic gifts, or even to his resurrection (though, it is true, Paul can speak of his being designated 'Son of God with power . . . by his resurrection from the dead'—Rom. 1:4). I should point the questioner rather to the Cross where he could see a love that is indestructible. Even when men flung it back in his face with derision, the flame of his love never flickered, but burned with unquenchable brilliance. Even when he knew himself deserted by God, and left to carry the weight of man's sin alone, in all the defencelessness of one who has no other weapon but love, his trust in God may have for a moment trembled, but his love for God never faltered. His agony was that he had been abandoned by the God who loved him and whom he loved. In the hour of his utmost need he received neither aid nor comfort, and yet his love never staggered. It was as sure, as total, in the complete darkness as it had been in the moment of deepest intimacy, for—and this is the paradox of faith—though he was abandoned yet he was not abandoned, and all unfelt, unknown, the power of the Father undergirded him. From the horns of the unicorns God heard him: not from some remote heaven where all is light and joy, but from the very heart of the darkness. 'If God had been there,' said the boy gazing at a picture of the crucifixion, 'he would not have let them do it.'[4] But it was only because God was there that it was allowed to happen. It was only because the Eternal Father had willed that the evil in man's heart should be conquered by the power of naked love, that the conflict ended at the Cross and in the demonstration that nothing can corrupt the love of the well-beloved Son. 'Truly this man was a son of God,' said the Roman centurion in awe, as he and his men watched Christ die with a shout of victory (Mark 15:39).

The obligation is laid on all Christians to love God and to love one another. Most would admit that their love of God is a curiously vague affair, and as for their fellow men, some they like, and some they dislike, while most they regard with a neutral indifference. But real love has very little to do with liking. 'Love,' wrote St Teresa, 'consists, not in the extent of our happiness, but in the firmness of our determination to try and please God in everything.'[5] Similarly we might say that love for our fellow men consists not so much in the extent of our liking for them, as in our firm determination to serve them and seek their good in all things. It is, therefore, fundamentally a matter of the will, and is to a very small extent dependent on the ebb and flow of our emotions. Even so, such a love in its heroic audacity is far beyond natural human strength, and is only achieved by the grace of God enabling us. There are a few who, when those whom they thought were their friends and whom they trusted implicitly, kick them in the teeth, as we expressively put it, still continue resolutely to serve them and seek their good. Through the malice of those they relied on, or it may be through their sheer stupidity, many have been brought to ruin, and though most of the victims may have nursed feelings of revenge, and hoped (and prayed even) for an opportunity to pay off old scores, yet some may have been able to go on serving with quiet determination. Many, through some accident, caused perhaps by the almost criminal carelessness of an acquaintance, have been maimed for life, or, what is more terrible, have been bereaved of some dear one. Some say, 'I will never forgive him. I will never speak to him again.' And if they should hear some day that the one who had wounded them so tragically was himself in some trouble where they could help, would feel only satisfaction that retribution had fallen on their enemy. A few, a very few, though they have been mangled by the horns of the unicorns, will go to help and if possible comfort these same unicorns when *they* are wounded and in dire straits. Of such is the Kingdom of Heaven.

In showing such steadfast love through all provocation and suffering, they express their love of God. Like their Saviour, when they suffer they utter no threats, but commit their cause to the One who judges justly, for that is the fundamental test of love—to suffer and yet still to be able to trust God: to feel yourself deserted by God, and left to the mercy of those who hate you, or overwhelmed by events that bring your life crashing about you in ruin, and yet know with quiet assurance that God is good and does all things well. Love is to be able to go on trusting when there is no evidence to justify trust. Here is love, to go down into the darkness and call to God for help, and get no reply: to cry to him and there is only silence, and yet to go on loving and trusting and serving. Here the believer's faith and love rise to their supreme heights and become fused with the victorious love of Christ, and in the very hour in which he finds himself abandoned and forsaken not by man only, but more terribly by God himself, if he still love and trust the God who allows him to pass through such agony, he will find God, not in spite of the darkness, but in the very heart of it. He will come to an awareness of God and an experience of his goodness and glory that pass far beyond anything he could have learned elsewhere. When he is gored by the horns of the unicorns, he will know that God has heard and answered him, and has indeed brought him to that very place that he might there give him the full wonders of his love. This is the way of the Cross. It can only be trodden in the strength of the crucified and victorious Saviour, but it leads to a peace and glory that can be found nowhere else.

EASTER

God brought them out of Egypt; he hath as it were
the strength of an unicorn. (Num. 23:22)

AT Christmas we meditated on the unicorn as the symbol of the Saviour
drawn down to earth by his love. On Good Friday we meditated on this
same unicorn as the symbol of the Redeemer who died for love—torn by
the horns of the unicorns. Now, as we reflect on Easter I would consider
the unicorn as the symbol of the sheer power of this Redeemer's love.

One of the strangest features of the unicorn, and the one which makes
it seem a most bizarre symbol for our Lord, is that it is so fierce and
dangerous that it cannot be tamed. It might seem a most wayward symbol
for the Saviour who would not cry nor lift up his voice nor make it heard
in the street: who would not break a bruised reed nor quench a dimly
smouldering light (cf. Isa. 42:2–3). We tend to think of Christ as the
embodiment of a love that is gentle and patient: that bears all things,
hopes all things and endures all things. But fierce? and dangerous? and
untamable? This scarcely enters into the conventional picture of Christ (or
even, come to that, into the conventional picture of Christian character).

When we read in the later Isaiah of the Servant of the Lord who was
wounded for our transgressions, we may too easily be misled by the symbolism of the lamb led to the slaughter into thinking of the Redeemer as
powerless to defend himself, a helpless victim in the hands of those who
wished him dead. This is clearly the simple explanation of the matter. The
cruel fate of the Redeemer is simply another example, perhaps the most
devastating proof there ever has been, that the universe is hostile to goodness, and is shaped only for the survival of the fittest—the fittest being the
most ruthless, who are prepared and able to fight for their survival. Yet
Holy Scripture does not write as the epitaph of our Lord,

> *Out, out brief candle!*
> *Life's but a walking shadow . . . a tale*
> *Told by an idiot, full of sound and fury,*
> *Signifying nothing.*[6]

It does not see in our Lord's death an unanswerable demonstration that there is no God at all, or if there is, that he cares nothing for the suffering of man, understandable enough though that conclusion might be. On the contrary, Scripture finds here triumphant evidence of the love of God, and what is even more surprising, finds such evidence only here. The reason plainly lies in the testimony of the first witnesses that Christ who had died upon the Cross was no longer dead, but was risen again by the power of God. The Gospel evidence is that the Cross was not God's last word. It was only the penultimate word. The last word is the Resurrection from the dead.

And so, though on Good Friday we sing of the Son of God hanging on the Cross, mocked by his enemies who exulted that though he had saved others he was powerless to save himself, on Easter day we see this in the light of the triumph of the Resurrection. In hymn after hymn we celebrate the victorious power by which the Son of God has conquered sin and death.

Hell and the grave combined their force,
To hold our Lord in vain;
Sudden the Conqueror arose,
And burst their feeble chain. [7]

The infinite power of God is never to be doubted. To think of him simply in terms of weakness and suffering and humiliation just will not do. That he is vulnerable beyond our imagining is shown in the shame and degradation of the Crucifixion, but, as Easter proclaims, he is the inexhaustible source of all energy and power. In his naked being he is dreadful in his omnipotence, and it was never the intention of the Christian faith to suggest anything else. We worship a God for whom all things are possible. The picture that is often painted of a God helplessly surveying the havoc and confusion of the world, and powerless to do anything about it; a God whose plans have been thwarted by the ingenuity of man and who has simply to submit, as we so often have to submit to the will of those who are stronger and more ruthless than we are, has in it something faintly ludicrous.

In fact, however, it is not at all ludicrous, but ominous. I have often felt that such a faithless attitude was little more than a theological dodge to rationalize the Church's own floundering incompetence. Certainly it is where the Church is in full retreat, with its membership falling and its worship becoming thinner and thinner, where it is tormented with the knowledge that it is little but a futile irrelevance because it has lost its faith—the faith that can move mountains—it is in that kind of situation that a theology of helplessness finds a congenial home. Yet the Church under the Cross is by no means the Church despairing. When Bonhoeffer in a famous passage writes, 'God lets himself be pushed out of the world on to the cross,'[8] the obvious retort is that if he was on the cross he was scarcely out of the world, but peculiarly involved in and with it. Paul is much nearer the heart of the matter when *he* writes, 'God was in Christ reconciling the world unto himself' (II Cor. 5:19). When, however, Bonhoeffer continues, 'He is weak and powerless in the world, and that is precisely the way, the only way, in which he is with us and helps us', there is no theological reply possible except to say that this is not true, and that it was not the faith by which Dietrich Bonhoeffer himself lived and died. The New Testament does not end with the Crucifixion but with the Resurrection, and every page flames with the note of the victory. Paul does not say, 'We can be thankful that God is as defeated as we are', but on the contrary, 'Thanks be to God who gives us the victory' (I Cor. 15:57). Holy Scripture is not a record of failure: it is the record of man's sin and of the sheer power of God's terrifying love. He has, in truth, the fierce, untamable strength of the unicorn, and when he puts forth his power to bring his people out of their spiritual bondage, there is no one who can stop his hand.

Paul Tillich is perfectly correct when he writes that we have today largely lost the sense of the abyss of the divine, of the unsearchable depths of God's power and glory and being. Our fathers knew what was meant by 'the fear of God', but we today do not. We have forgotten what makes God God.

The first principle is the basis of Godhead, that which makes God God. It is the root of his majesty, the unapproachable intensity of his being, the inexhaustible ground of being in which everything has its origin. It is the power of being infinitely resisting non-being, giving the power of being to everything that is. During the past centuries theological and philosophical rationalism have deprived the idea of God of this first principle, and by doing so they have robbed God of his divinity. He has become a hypostasised moral ideal or another name for the structural unity of reality. The power of the Godhead has disappeared.[9]

The primordial strength and energy of the Unicorn, laughing his enemies to scorn, has by sentimental thinking been drained away, until we have been left with a gentle and ineffectual God, who makes so little difference to the world that it scarcely matters whether there is a God at all. We seem no longer to understand either the creative or the destructive power of God's love; it can be stern, it can be relentless, it can be very terrible.

14

There is in it an energy that we underestimate to our cost, a sheer power that laughs at obstacles and scatters opposition.

Love without power is only a sentimental emotion. Indeed, life without power is a mere shadow of life. It is one of the conditions of life that we have to struggle if we are to achieve our aims, and this we cannot hope to do unless there is within us a driving force, an energy, a power. Some have this more than others naturally, but we all have some inner power by which we face life and wrestle with the angel of destiny. If we have not, we merely drift where the tide carries us, and are, in the good Scots word, fusionless, that is, lacking in all drive and vitality. Now the source from which all power comes ultimately is the living God, the great deep of inexhaustible energy, and to speak of God as limited in power is to speak of a finite God, which is a mere contradiction in terms and therefore meaningless. One word that should never be used when we are speaking of God is the word 'impossible'. With God all things are possible, said our Lord (Mark 10:27), and he was not speaking loosely, but meant what he said.

All things are possible to God, but within the terms of his eternal will and purpose. It is not thinkable that for the sake of a cheap and easy victory in the immediate event he should destroy the goal towards which he works. We are told that he has made man in his own image and likeness (Gen. 1:26—27), therefore he cannot, because he will not, use means that would destroy in man that very image in which he was made. That is to say that in all his dealings with the souls of men he will never use force to destroy their freedom and coerce them into obedience, far less into love. The eternal Spirit of God is free, determined by nothing outside of himself, and were he to use that force with the world and with us that some zealous souls would like to see him use (and that we ourselves in some of our moods would almost welcome his using against ourselves), then, whatever the initial gain might be, or seem to be, he should have destroyed in us our freedom and our dignity, thus destroying that very image of himself which it is his purpose to perfect. In dealing with the souls of men the fierce, creative energy of the love of God, just because it is love, will not take us without our willing surrender, for if it did, that would be rape which would destroy the very blessedness he has purposed for us. Here his love must wait with a patience that is as terrifying as his sheer power, until the wonder of his beauty and goodness conquer us by gentleness, and until his truth works its own acceptance and is freely acknowledged. He must stoop to conquer.

But the power is never in question, never for an instant. On Easter morning the Saviour who had died for love was raised from the dead by the power of the love of God, to die no more, and to him has been given all power in heaven and in earth. 'Jesus has vanquished death and all its powers.'[10] That is the beginning of the Good News of Easter, the glorious message we have to proclaim: glorious, but not incredible. Why should it be thought incredible that God can do such things? The fierce, untamable unicorn is victorious over death, death which seems so final, so unconquerable, death that men fight and struggle against and fear, but to which everyone must inevitably submit. Yet to God it is neither final nor inevitable. If death has any power—as it clearly has—that power itself must come from God who is the source of all power, and therefore even death is completely subject to him. God who can do all things brought the Saviour out from the bondage of death and corruption. 'He hath as it were the strength of an unicorn.'

Yet that is only the beginning of the story. There are many who would rest there and ask no more, content to have the assurance that death is not the end of human existence, and happy enough to continue into an infinite future the life that they know in this world. Paul is wiser. His longing is not so much that he may never die, as that he may be made a new man. He would know not only the fact of Christ's resurrection but also its power, for as Lightfoot says, 'The essence of knowing Christ consists in knowing the power of His resurrection.'[11] Jesus had vanquished death, but let him now by the power of his resurrection vanquish the proud, stubborn heart of Paul. This was what amazingly happened, and Paul, the narrow Pharisee, who had believed in the use of force to stamp out the new and heretical faith, who had been hard and merciless in his righteousness, hating all that Christ had stood for as suffering, humiliated love, had himself been laid hold on by Christ in such a way that he who had been revolted by the very idea of a crucified Messiah was himself crucified with Christ, the old Paul dying in repentance and becoming only a memory, and yet he was alive as he had never been before—but it was not he who was alive, but Christ living in him. Christ had conquered him by love, and the wonder of it never left him: as he told the Galatians, 'the life which I now live in the flesh I live by the faith of the Son of God, who loved me, and gave himself for me' (Gal. 2:20). Here are held in unbroken unity the power of God which *cannot* be defeated and the love of God which never *is*.

So at Easter we rejoice not only that the power of death has been broken, but fully as much that the power of evil and suffering to darken life has also been broken and that the way has been opened to us into a new and glorious future. When God brought his people out of bondage in Egypt, he did not leave then to wander aimlessly round in circles in an unfriendly desert, and we can be sure that having delivered his people from the even greater bondage of death, he does not leave them to drift for ever in the old futile, unsatisfying, self-centred and loveless existence which is all that they have known. He makes possible for them a new life of creative love like his own. For there is in Christ's love a boundless power before which devils tremble and the powers of darkness crumble. Time's glory, said the poet, is 'to tame the unicorn and lion wild,'[12] but not even time can sap the power of the eternal love of God, and it is to no ineffectual Saviour that we turn, confident that he will sympathize with us even if he cannot do much to help, but to the creative source of all life against which evil may struggle, but which it can never hope to overcome.

There is nothing that can curb the power of God except his own love. One of the loveliest of the unicorn tapestries in the Cloisters in New York City shows the unicorn shut in an enclosure. The animal is vibrating with life and energy, and our first thought is surely that so active a creature cannot possibly be confined by a fence that it could step over without even the trouble of jumping. But as we ponder, we come to sense that it is only held there because that is what it itself wishes. It is its own love that holds it, and in all its beauty, restrained power quivering in every limb, it rests there captive. The captive of love held by invisible chains.

'All power is liable to corrupt', Lord Acton wrote to a friend, 'and absolute power corrupts absolutely'.[13] That is sadly true, as the history of the world has shown again and again, but it is true only up to a point. When power is controlled by love, it will corrupt neither him who wields it nor those who are subject to it, and absolute power controlled by absolute love is the final security of mankind. The unicorn is so fierce and powerful that the boldest hunter cannot tame it, and yet love draws it in self-sacrificing gentleness whither it will. This is the basis of all Christian faith, that the power of God can do all things, and that the love of God can be utterly trusted, and that in God these are not two things but a perfect unity.

ASCENSION DAY

*For my sword shall be bathed in heaven: behold it shall come down
upon Idumea, and upon the people of my curse, to judgement. . . . And
the unicorns shall come down with them, and the bullocks with the
bulls; . . . For it is the day of the Lord's vengeance, and the year
of recompences for the controversy of Zion. (Isa. 34:5–8)*

THE times in which we live are indeed the day of the Lord's vengeance,
and men's hearts are failing them for fear of the things that may be coming
on the earth. The Lord has a controversy with the nations, and his judgements hang heavy over the peoples. The path of greed and lust and envy,
of selfishness and arrogance, of hypocrisy and lies, of injustice and cruelty
and war, may be followed for a long time without obvious disaster, but of
this we may be sure: that one day the reckoning will have to be paid, and
paid in full to the last farthing. Men may fight and struggle with all their
ingenuity, they may devise the most brilliant of schemes to save themselves, but the more they struggle the more they become entangled in the
web of their own folly and sin. Every day is the day of God's mercy and
grace: that is never to be doubted. But every day, it seems to me, must
also be a day of God's vengeance, for the Lord who is the God of justice
and love must, being what he is, be utter destruction to all that is loveless
and evil. That is why this passage of Isaiah is heavy with doom. The indignation of the Lord is upon all nations, and his fury upon all their armies.
He has utterly destroyed them, he has delivered them to the slaughter.
Even the gentle Jeremiah goes further and sees that there is no exemption
for the People of God in the coming ruin, and he prophesies: 'You must
and shall drink [the cup of my fury]. I will first punish the city that bears
my name; do you think that you can be exempt? . . . Ruin spreads from
nation to nation, a mighty tempest is blowing up from the ends of the earth'
(Jer. 25: 29, 32 NEB). Later or sooner, the finger comes forth and writes
on the plaster of the wall against a civilization of sordid greed and blatant
materialism, 'Thou art weighed in the balances, and art found wanting'
(Dan. 5:27).

Nothing is here for our comfort, you may say, and perhaps it is so.

> *I tell you naught for your comfort,*
> *Yea, naught for your desire,*
> *Save that the sky grows darker yet*
> *And the sea rises higher.* [14]

Yet the surprising thing is that the grim threats of the prophet do not issue in despair but in promise. For the mercy of God always has the last word, and precisely at this point of utter darkness the symbolism of the unicorn shows its significance again: this strange symbol of the Christ who is so terrible that a conflict with him can only end in defeat, but who yet accepts without reservation the claims and the appeal of love, and surrenders himself to the sinful and helpless, allowing himself to be slain with impunity by his enemies, the ruthless hunters, as another of the Cloisters tapestries starkly depicts. Certainly the unicorn is a fierce creature that it is fatal—and futile—to attack, and yet this prophecy of Isaiah suggests strange thoughts. The sword of the Lord will not only come down on the enemies of Israel, but (as Amos and Jeremiah saw clearly) it will fall even on Israel itself, and what is more awesome yet, it shall be bathed in blood in heaven. It may be that the Hebrew text here ought to be emended, but as we are using the passage simply as a basis from which meditation on fundamental Christian teaching can grow, it may be allowed to stand as it is—'My sword shall be bathed [i.e. in blood] in heaven . . . and the unicorn shall be slain along with the evil doer in the day of the Lord's vengeance.' 'Where is the lamb for a burnt offering?' Isaac asked his father Abraham, as they climbed up Mount Moriah, and Abraham replied confidently (or perhaps, being human, only evasively) 'My son, God will provide himself a lamb for a burnt offering' (cf. Gen. 22:1—14).

So it is that when the judgements of God are abroad in the earth, it is upon the Son of his love, and therefore on himself, that the doom falls. The drama of our redemption begins in heaven; that is to say, it begins in eternity in the realm of ultimate reality, and it is upon the heavenly unicorn that the bitter weight of man's sin falls. The price is paid in heaven before ever it is paid on earth. The Lamb of God has taken away the sins of the world in heaven, and the Cross set up on Calvary makes visible, and makes part of human history, the eternal sacrificial love of God.

On the Feast of the Ascension we rejoice that this redemption, though in a real sense once and for all and complete, is still a present reality. In the words of the Creed, Christ our Lord 'was crucified, dead, and buried. . . . The third day he rose again from the dead, he ascended into

19

heaven, and sitteth on the right hand of God the Father Almighty.' What can this mean? Simply that Christ had indubitably been dead, but he was living again, but not visibly among his disciples, for after the briefest of reunions, in the phrase of Karl Barth, 'before their eyes He ceased to be before their eyes.'[15] It is pointless to ask where he went or how he went. We simply do not have data to answer that kind of question. It was sufficient for the disciples to know, in words which whether completely authentic or not, undoubtedly express the unshakable faith of the early Church, that all power was given to him in heaven and on earth, and that he would be with them always to the end of time (cf. Mat. 28:18). Calvin is perfectly correct when he insists that the Ascension of our Lord is not to be understood as his withdrawal into peace and blessedness when the conflict was over, but rather that all power is now in his hands, and that everything is placed at his disposal.[16] The fundamental fact upon which all history turns, though so few may know it, and even fewer believe it, is that the destiny, and therefore the control, of the entire universe lies in the pierced hands of the ascended Christ. His eternal victory was revealed in time at the cross and at the empty tomb, but it is not at the mercy of the chances of time, nor can it be assailed by the malice of his enemies.

Thus the drama of the unicorn ends in heaven where it had first begun. The Ascension, like the Cross and the Resurrection, is an event in eternity which penetrates this world of space and time at one particular point, and yet, because it is eternal, is contemporary with each and every moment. For that reason, though it is an historical event, it is vastly more significant than any merely historical event. We are concerned here with the ultimate realities, with that which lies behind all that is passing, with what is final, unchanging and unchangeable. It is not with a dead Christ that we confront men, but with a living and ascended Christ, and we tell them both for their comfort and for their warning that part of the reality of their existence, with which they have to reckon and with which they have to come to terms, is that the ascended Christ reigns, and reigns victoriously, and reigns for ever. There is no escape for anyone from the challenge of the Cross, and equally there is no escape from the challenge of the Resurrection and the Ascension. Whether we like it or not, this is something we can neither change, nor reason away, nor laugh out of court. We may well be in rebellion against the Lordship of Christ, but if we are, we are only (as Paul learned long ago) kicking against the pricks. The ascended Christ, whose love cannot be either killed or fettered, lives and acts over against our every action, and we cannot alter the realities of the

20

universe, though we can and do make our own wounds deeper, and the problems in which we are entangled more intractable.

Yet it is for our comfort that we are not, or we need not be, abandoned to our own resources. Christ ascended is not a Saviour who has washed his hands of the task. 'I have done all that I can be expected to do; now get on with it yourselves.' He stands to his promise that in a mysterious yet very real way he would be with his followers to the very end. Christ ascended is not Christ departed, and Christ invisible is not Christ ineffective. When he died upon the Cross God was not edged out of the world, but a power was let loose in the world whose effects have been incalculable; and though there are periods, certainly, when its energy seems to have been exhausted, yet such periods can be deceptive. Up till now they have always been the prelude to a new and unprecedented explosion, and I see no ground for thinking that things will be different in the future.

Here we are moving in realms of titanic dimensions. Certainly, the Crucifixion and the events which followed it can be discussed by the secular historians in purely human terms. It is often enough done. Yet it is not so that the New Testament understands them, and it is to something more than human that it bears witness. In the great act of the redemption and the perfecting of the whole creation the beginning lies with God, and the end lies with God, and all that lies between is of God also. The battle is God's, and the victory is his. It is by no means an idyllic story, full of light and sweetness all the way. The darkness is very real, and the pain and cruelty in the world are very real also, and these things have tormented the minds of the thoughtful from the earliest times. There is black mystery here that it is dishonesty to deny and only folly to ignore. Yet behind all that happens stands the fact that Christ is victorious and that he is on the throne of the universe.

I find myself wondering, as I listen to the gloomy forebodings of the faint-hearted, whether the Church has forgotten that the eternal destiny of all souls is guided and overruled by a love whose power is quite beyond our comprehension, and that whatever happens, however often we fail, whatever suffering or sorrow may come, however the pattern of things with which we are familiar and feel safe may change, we are called upon to trust the love of Christ that passes knowledge. For that love is still real, still fierce, and still suffering, and reigns for ever.

The Church—at least the Reformed Church—in this century seems to have grown increasingly confused as to the nature of its own existence. The visible Church, with its opportunities and its mission to serve the world, it recognizes: it is also well aware of its impotence and its ineptitude, to say nothing of its cowardice. The invisible Church, in all its power and glory, seems to be beyond its comprehension. At all events, it is not part of the reality with which we have to reckon in our daily life, and though we may give it lip-service for the sake of keeping up appearances, it may for practical purposes be ignored. Is not this to throw away the essence of our existence as a Church? Has the centre of gravity in the Church not shifted dangerously when it has been allowed to slide from the invisible to the visible? And is the implication of such a shift not that the things which are seen are real, but that the things which are not seen are only visionary? Yet our Lord made it plain enough that the centre of gravity of human life lay deep in the unseen. It was from there that all *his* power came. He was indeed often most active when visibly he seemed doing least, and it has been well said that he did more for his people when he was alone with God in the silence of the night, pacing the hills of Galilee, than during the day in the dust and noise of the village streets. But whether in the night or in the day, he was the centre of the battle, and the Church must not allow itself to forget—unless it is content to become a meaningless irrelevancy—that its true life is hid with Christ in God. Where he is, the real battle is still being fought, and it is there that the real victories are won. That is to say, the Church is other-worldly, not in the sense that it has drifted away from the realities of existence to some comfortable haven where the noises of a vulgar world scarcely reach it, but in the sense that in this world it witnesses to, and draws upon, a power that is not of this world.

The power of the unicorn still reigns in the affairs of men. The unicorn has not been tamed and he cannot be tamed. In the very fact that he is ascended, and therefore beyond our reach and our control, lies his danger to all that is evil and against love. He cannot be domesticated, far less caged—not even by those who love him, and certainly not by the sentimental. Writing to the Christians in Ephesus, Paul reminds them of the glory of the ascended Christ, but even more of the power of the ascended Christ which is incalculable and which fills the whole universe, and on which all who believe can draw without limit. He writes,

God has placed everything under the power of Christ and has set Him up as Head of everything for the Church. For the Church is His body, and in that body lives fully the One Who fills the whole wide universe.
(Eph. 1: 22–23, J.B. Phillips, 1947 edn.)

PENTECOST

He maketh them also to skip like a calf; Lebanon
and Sirion like a young unicorn.   (Ps. 29: 6)

A CURIOUS feature of the legend of the unicorn was the belief in the dual properties of its horn. A wound from the horn of the unicorn, it was thought, was almost always fatal, or at the least extremely dangerous. This was to be expected, for the unicorn was fierce and untamable, and its horn which men found lying on the ground—and which was really the ivory tusk of the narwhal, one of the whale family—was three to four foot long, and tapered to a fine point. (In fact, the narwhal has never been known to attack anybody with its tusk, but the human imagination is capable of great flights.) So people shuddered at the thought of being transfixed by this ferocious weapon. Yet, at the same time, it was believed that this fatal horn possessed remarkable virtue, and if dipped in any poisonous liquid at once rendered it safe to drink. This legend was firmly believed as late as the reign of Charles II, and in France until the Revolution instruments made of unicorn's horn were still used to safeguard the king's food.

There is no difficulty in understanding how the unicorn, whose horn could by its inherent power make poisonous things wholesome, might very fittingly be used as a symbol of the Saviour who had himself such creative, cleansing power that even to touch the hem of his garment was sufficient to bring healing. But did those who laid hold on this vivid symbol overlook, very conveniently, that this same health-bringing horn was also horrifyingly destructive? I do not think so. They understood that life and death are separated by the narrowest of lines: that the same substances can bring either healing or death, depending on how they are used, and that some of the most valuable medicines in the Pharmacopoeia can, when ignorantly used, be fatal. They knew that the rays of the sun which can nourish life can also bring death. They knew, what so many today do not seem to know, that books which can be read by some without risk and indeed with spiritual enrichment, spell nothing but death to the souls of others: that

23

truly one man's meat can be another's poison. So they found nothing incongruous in using the unicorn, this destructive creature, the touch of whose horn could, none the less, transform the death-dealing into the life-giving, as a symbol for the Saviour.

For is it not the case that though for multitudes Christ has meant cleansing from all that was poisoning their lives, yet to many he seems only to have brought the hardening of their hearts? He was for many the Great Physician: he went about doing good: he spoke as no man had ever spoken before. The writer of the Fourth Gospel could declare that he was full of grace and truth, and that he, and many others had seen his glory, glory as of the only Son from the Father. Yet others could see in him only a blasphemer of God, threatening everything that they held most dear. To some the unicorn brought healing and a new purity of life, but to others he brought only death. All down the ages this has been the tragic impact of Christ upon man, an impact not of his making, far less of his desiring, but in the nature of things inevitable. From the very beginning he has divided men to the right and to the left, for some have believed and some have rejected him. To Peter he brought life; to Judas death. The unicorn is perhaps a truer symbol of the Eternal Saviour than we are altogether willing to acknowledge. In him is both life and death, and though we should cling fast to the promise, yet we should be foolish to forget, or treat lightly, the warning.

A deeper mystery yet lies hidden here, for it is the strange work of the Saviour first to kill and then through death to bring new life. 'Come, let us return to the Lord; for he has torn, that he may heal us; he has stricken, and he will bind us up. After two days he will revive us; on the third day he will raise us up, that we may live before him' (Hos. 6:1–2 RSV). The horn of the unicorn: life and death united. There is a significant detail in the story of the curing of Naaman's leprosy which is not always noticed. When Naaman was sent to the king of Israel to be cured, we read that the king rent his garments and cried out, 'Am I God, to kill and to make alive' (2 Kgs. 5: 7). It is, on the face of it, an odd exclamation, for no one was asking him to kill anyone, but simply to have a man cured of leprosy. Yet he gives involuntary testimony to the awfulness of God who both kills and makes alive: who makes alive often by killing.

This St Paul was to discover. He was a Pharisee, passionately righteous, a lover of the Law of God as he understood it, and consequently consumed with a blind hatred of Jesus of Nazareth and of all who followed him. Filled with what he considered a righteous and almost divine fury, he believed himself appointed by God to destroy this new sect utterly. If we did not know the end of the story, we should have said that he suffered from invincible blindness, and was incapable of seeing the glory of Christ. But we know that on the road to Damascus he was struck down in all his pride, and was led by the hand into the city a shattered man. Christ had met him on the Damascus road in love and in judgement, and had shown that he was indeed God to kill and to make alive. Paul died in that hour and a new man was born. I grant that there are philosophical puzzles here. How can you become a new man, a different man, and still display many of the characteristics of the man who died? How can you be recognizably the same person, and yet be changed, as we say, beyond recognition? We can only answer that the thing happens. Certainly for Paul the matter was real enough, and his own explanation was that from that day it was not he who lived but Christ who lived in him. We shall never begin to understand his passionate theology unless we see that it all stems from that day and from that death. Indeed, I think, truly to understand the letters of St Paul it is not theological learning that is required, but to have been done to death by Christ as he was done to death. The unicorn must slay us before he can heal us. It is not necessarily a violent death in agony as Paul's was. Death is not always painful and humiliating: it can be very gentle and peaceful. But death there must be. The old man must cease to exist in order that the new man may be born and slowly grow to maturity. We must die with Christ if we would live with him.

Here we approach the miracle of Pentecost, for Pentecost is the miracle of new life. In the words of the Creed, 'We believe in the Holy Spirit, the Lord, the giver of life.' The gifts of the Spirit are endless. Traditional theology speaks of the seven gifts of the Spirit. Seven? Seventy times seven might be a wiser estimate, but the wisest of all is to put no limits to his creative generosity. The fundamental gift, however, is the gift of new life—the life of the Risen and Glorified Saviour, who through the communion of the Holy Spirit dwells in us and we in him, so that the life that we lead is no longer our own life, but is more properly called his life.

A superficial reading of the events of the day of Pentecost might lead us to suppose that the work of the Spirit was to create excitement, enthusiasm and tumult: the rushing wind, the tongues of fire, the crowd flocking from all over the city, and the disciples talking an unspecified language that everyone understood in his own native tongue (cf Acts 2: 1–13). In times of religious renewal such outbreaks are not unknown, and they are certainly not to be sneered at, but the essence of the Spirit does not lie in emotional disturbance. As a distinguished bishop once remarked, somewhat sourly, 'The Holy Spirit must not be confused with high spirits', but then neither should he be confused with low spirits as he so often seems to be. His power is inward and his influence most silent. After all, he is not a spirit of confusion, but is a still, small voice. His characteristic work is to unite the soul with Christ, to kill the self-oriented man whose finest actions are still tinged with self-love, and to create in him the new life which is Christ dwelling in his heart through faith and love.

For it is a *new life*. It may not be very different in outward appearance from the old life, for after all is said, it is a hidden life—hidden with Christ in God—even though the classical examples that are continually cited are those of St Paul and St Mary Magdalene, because they show the change in its most dramatic and most easily recognized form. In line with this, an hundred years ago preachers found their typical illustration of the changed life in the converted drunkard. Such examples of the grace of God are miracles never to be belittled, but many new lives are much less spectacular, though equally miraculous.

It is a new life because its centre and its driving force lie in the Holy Spirit. This is probably the greatest difference between religion and politics. Both wish to change the world, but the politician has to take people as they are, and try to build a new world with such materials as lie to his hand. Religion seeks to create new people, for it knows that to create a new world the essential thing is to have new people, otherwise the injustice repressed in one direction will break out, perhaps with greater virulence, in some other, and in the end of the day things will be much the same as they have always been, and the dream of humanity still only a dream.

This is also the fundamental distinction between most moral reforms and the new life of the Spirit. A moral reform seeks to lift what is already there to a higher level, to purify it of faults, to point it, perhaps, in a different direction. It may succeed beyond all expectation, but there can be one quite fatal consequence. It tends to rivet the attention of the soul on the self and its achievements. In the last resort everything still revolves round the self and its fulfilment, and even love of the neighbour becomes a refined self-love. In such cases defeat is often more profitable to the soul than victory, for we can so pride ourselves on the victories that we win that we become Pharisees, since the essence of a Pharisee is that his goodness is conscious. He is not a man who pretends to be better than he really is: he is one who is truly upright, but who is well aware of the fact, and can even with all sincerity thank God for it. But how can a Christian possibly be a

Pharisee? It is the life of Christ that lives in him. His own life is no more. It is of Christ that he is conscious, not of himself. It is worth pondering that in the Parable of the Sheep and the Goats (cf. Mat. 25: 31–46), none were more astonished than those whom Christ set at his right hand. What have we ever done, they asked, to merit this? Whatever filled the centre of their thoughts, it was not the contemplation of themselves.

We may sum up by saying that the Christian, as Henry Drummond long ago pointed out, is eccentric.[17] He lives with a new centre to his existence when by the power of the Holy Spirit he is made one with Christ and lives no longer unto himself but unto him who died for us and rose again. Through love of his own the heavenly Unicorn was drawn into this world not only that he might destroy all that enslaved us and robbed life of its glory, but that he might also give us his own life in so intimate a union that dying to ourselves we become for the first time truly ourselves. We become real and individualized as we had never been before. Those in whom Christ lives do not, as some seem to imagine, become as alike as peas in a pod. St Paul, St Francis of Assisi and Elizabeth Fry are completely distinguishable, and no one could ever mistake one of them for another. Yet each of them died and in them all Christ lived as their true life, the centre from which all that was most distinctive flowed.

A set of four tapestries in the Cloisters in New York depicts the hunting of the unicorn. One of them shows the unicorn kneeling at a stream that gushes from an ornate fountain, dipping its horn into the water and so purifying it. Round it stand many wild creatures waiting to drink safely, while in the background are the hunters with their weapons and hounds. Most take this simply as a very lovely picture of the unicorn purifying the water that it may be safe to drink, but for myself I am convinced that it is much more enigmatic than that. This is the end of the hunt, not the beginning, and the unicorn is mortally wounded, but even as it dies, its horn trailing in the water brings cleansing. Death and life come together again, and it is in dying that the unicorn purifies the stream issuing from the Temple threshold, which as Ezekiel foresaw (cf. Ezek. 47: 1–12), would be the source of life to all: 'every thing shall live whither the river cometh'. It is by dying that the unicorn brings life, and it is by incorporating us into that death that he gives us his eternal life. As the Fourth Gospel says, it is not until Jesus is glorified—crucified, risen and ascended—that the Holy Spirit can be given, the Spirit who is the Lord of Life (John 7: 39).

The twenty-ninth psalm from which the text of this meditation has been taken has been called the Psalm of the Seven Thunders. Seven times the

27

voice of the Lord peals forth like thunder from the black storm clouds, while the forked lightning strikes down to shatter the majestic cedars and to make even the mighty mountains Lebanon and Sirion (i.e. Hermon) quake. Yet this psalm is much more than a picture of the terrible majesty of God and the helplessness of frail humanity, for it has an unexpected ending; at least it would be unexpected if we did not know the mystery of Christ. For the final word is not devastation and destruction, but blessing. Opening with a vision of the power of God before which all things tremble, it ends: 'The Lord will give strength unto his people; the Lord will bless his people with peace.' The last word of God is never vengeance and destruction, but always love. The power and glory of God shine at their brightest in the reshaping and renewal of his shattered creation, and all things wait for that day in which they shall share in the joy and peace of which he gave a pledge to the Church at Pentecost. It was the promise of Christ that he would make all things new, and at the last the prophecy of the Book of Genesis will be fulfilled, 'And God saw everything that he had made, and behold, it was very good' (cf. Rev. 21: 5 & Gen. 1: 31).

FEAST OF THE TRANSFIGURATION

For the good will of him that dwelt in the bush: let the blessing
come upon the head of Joseph, and upon the top of the head
of him that was separated from his brethren. His glory is like
the firstling of his bullock, and his horns are like
the horns of unicorns. (Deut. 33: 16–17)

THE GLORY of the unicorn draws man like a magnet. For all the danger, perhaps because of the danger, men hunt it down remorselessly, even though they may suspect that they can never, for all their skill and boldness, capture it, and though the only thing that they can do with it, should it put itself in their power, is to kill it. They have never clearly seen it, for they can never come near it, and at best it is a dim white shape, leading them in a wild pursuit through valleys and over hills.

O Unicorn among the Cedars
To whom no magic charm can lead us. [18]

So man in his spiritual life strives onwards and upwards towards the ideal which indeed he faintly sees, but which he can never reach because it flies before him, seldom completely out of sight, but never even remotely within his grasp. The history of mankind is most truly understood as being from the beginning a groping—it is seldom more—after a dimly sensed perfection. It is the unending quest for truth, for beauty, and for goodness. Sometimes he imagines that he has found what he sought, that the goal has been won, and that he can now enjoy the triumph of achievement, only to discover that he has made but one small step forward and that the end is not even in sight. The quest is by no means uninterrupted, but both for the individual and for the race it is far oftener a history of painful advance, followed by a period when matters simply stand still, if there is not indeed a recession to ways that we thought we had conquered and left behind us for ever. It is difficult to see why advance should not be continuous, even if slow, but whether explicable or not, reality has to be faced, and we have to reckon with long, dreary periods of decadence and the repudiation of much wisdom that our ancestors valued. It is our tragedy that so often, and by so many, such periods of reversion to the primitive and to wallowing in the primeval mud are justified with intellectual brilliance and no small wit, on the unspoken assumption that the ideal which men have been seeking has no reality, and that the pursuit of it is mere folly. It can sound mightily impressive, but it is often little more than what F.H. Bradley called 'phrases behind which shallowness tries to look like wisdom.'[19]

Yet once the ideal took form and lived among men, a part of human history that cannot be shrugged off but remains to be the hope of all human striving and the judgement upon all human love of mediocrity and the easy way. Whenever men have really been confronted by Christ, they have felt the challenge of his perfection, and though some have hated, some have loved. 'There is that in his face that we would fain call master', and far beyond reason and logic we know that here is all perfection beyond which it is impossible to go. Here we touch God himself, and blindly, blunderingly we follow.

They who understand not cannot forget, and they
Who keep not his commandment call him Master and Lord.[20]

Christ is so demanding, and yet so patient. He claims from his followers everything—the whole of their life, and yet he will accept and bless the half-grudged little that they are willing to give, and he is so gentle with them and only severe when severity will help them best. At the heart of his goodness to us there lies a terrifying self-giving, as though even he had no right to claim all from us unless he had given all for us. He strides through the world so far ahead of us that we cannot catch him up, and yet we follow because in a dark world it is only in the brilliance of his light that we have any comfort. Here is the one human life that is truly human, and yet it is more than human. This is a life that is supremely natural, and yet it is more than that—it is supernatural.

Shortly before he went up to Jerusalem where he knew that he would be rejected and put to death, our Lord, accompanied by only three of his disciples went up a mountain that he might have silence and solitude to pray. As he prayed, we read, he was transfigured and his whole body shone with light. Even his clothing seemed to gleam—like snow in moonlight. It must be admitted that this whole incident causes embarrassment to Western scientific minds. Many preachers and commentators evade the issue by treating it as a vision in the overstrained minds of the disciples. Most writers simply ignore it. In the Eastern Orthodox Church it is a subject of constant meditation, but not in the West. If it is not dismissed as a vision, it is usually assumed, so far as I can see, that it was some kind of miracle worked for the benefit of the disciples, to help them to hold fast and still trust in their Lord when he was betrayed and crucified. It may well have been so, and yet I think not, or not primarily. Our Saviour went up into the mountain to pray, and not to make a display. As he prayed his whole appearance was transformed, but this was not so much a revelation of the hidden divinity as the glorification of his human life by its intense communion with the uncreated glory of God. It was indeed the revelation of the final goal of humanity—what it was created to be, and what by the grace of God it will ultimately come to be. Here is the end of all human striving. Here is man as seen by God in the Kingdom of his glory.

> *O wondrous type, O vision fair*
> *Of glory that the Church shall share.* [21]

Though, like everything in our Lord's life, this transformation is unique to him, and in our present state at least, far, if not infinitely, beyond anything that we can experience, yet it is not without approximations among those whose life of prayer and communion with God is intense and passionate with love. We read that when Moses came down from the mountain after talking for forty days with God his face shone with an unearthly light (cf. Exod. 34: 29–35). The New Testament says little on the subject, but is there, I find myself wondering, a hint of it in the first chapter of the second century *Acts of Paul and Thecla*, where in the description of Paul's appearance (so unflattering that it must surely have historical foundation) we read, 'Sometimes he appeared as a man, sometimes he had the countenance of an angel.' The Orthodox Church can provide many examples, but there is no need for us to look so far afield. All who are familiar with the life of St Columba can recall the account of the death of that holy man: how on the night when he died, as he was praying alone in the church, the other monks saw the whole building filled with brilliant light which gradually faded as they ran to it. Entering, they found the saint lying before the altar, still alive but at the point of death, and with his face still bright with an unearthly joy.[22]

It is not always easy, and perhaps it is not wise to try to separate truth from poetic legend in many of these accounts of transfiguration, but there is one thing in them all that never changes and is abundantly clear. The transfiguration of the body is never mentioned for its own sake. What is of importance is the surpassing holiness of the transfigured person and the glory of his communion with God. It is here that the essential glory lies, and the physical transformation is seen simply as an accompaniment, almost an inevitable accompaniment. For there must be no mistake here.

The meaning and purpose of human life is an ever deepening communion with God, and without this, all human achievement is still poverty, an unsatisfied craving for what alone can complete existence and give it meaning.

By no means the least puzzling mystery of human life is the way in which physical and spiritual unite in one homogeneous entity. It comes naturally to us to think of spirit and matter as completely different, and we cannot imagine how they unite and interpenetrate. Eastern philosophy tends to solve the problem by assuming that the visible, material universe is illusion above which the wise man must rise to have his existence in the world of the spirit which alone is real. In the West the tendency is rather to try and narrow the gulf between them, if not indeed to deny any fundamental difference at all. So we find every kind of theory, ranging from pure materialism which treats mind and spirit as only forms of matter, through every shade of hypothesis to pure idealism in which matter is only a form or manifestation of spirit. Yet, sooner of later every theory that has been suggested has broken down, and I am afraid that the ordinary person simply treats the two as completely different, uses them both, and does not trouble himself very much about the problems of such an odd state of affairs.

Yet if they are so disparate, how does it happen that this body thinks thoughts beyond the reach of time and space, and how does this immaterial spirit suffer from the agonies of toothache—and from torments much worse? It is fortunate that we do not have to explain life before we start living it. If it is a mystery, it is one that we all live, some of us very badly, some reasonably successfully, and a few—alas, only a few—with fine glory. Yet whether we do it well or ill, we live in both worlds, and, I suspect, never contrive to live in the one to the exclusion of the other.

Blessed be God, said Moses, for the good will of him that dwelt in the bush. Blessed be he who so created matter that it is a home for spirit: that each can inhabit the other without either being destroyed or stripped of its essential qualities. The bush, we read, burned with fire, and yet it was not consumed (Exod. 3: 2). That could of course happen. The fire may destroy the bush, or the bush may suffocate the fire. Neither, however, need happen, and God himself can be incarnate in his creation without that creation disintegrating in ruin.

Once again we see the glory of the unicorn who reconciles in himself so many opposites. Our Saviour is the Eternal Word who by his incarnation has united in himself both heaven and earth. In him God and man are become one, and while the Godhead has not annihilated the manhood or made it less than real, the manhood has not diminished the unique and

32

solitary majesty of God. For two thousand years the restless minds of theologians have been trying to solve this mystery, or at least give a rational explanation of it, but it is, I suspect, humanly insoluble. Either the incarnate presence of God fades into a vague, spiritual influence, or the very human man dissolves into an insubstantial ghost. But the truth remains, and by it believers live, that the Lord dwelt in the bush and the bush was not consumed.

It is astonishing what an intensity of spirit matter is able to sustain. Under normal, or what pass for normal, conditions there are of course limits. The great creative artists have often worn their bodies out prematurely. Again and again too mighty a spirit has inhabited too frail a body, though indeed I often wonder whether the spirit does not burn more brightly in a frail body than in one that is robust. But passing that by, we must note to our shame that human flesh and blood can support an intensity of spiritual life far beyond anything that our normal lukewarm and very conventional religion ever dreams of. Watching on the Mount of Transfiguration with Peter and James and John, we must surely learn that human life is of such a kind that it can be raised to unimagined heights by communion with God.

The pursuit of material security, the struggle to win an ever increasing control of the material resources of the world, the search for affluence and comfort and ease, have always been characteristics of human history. They are not an invention of the twentieth century. It would be easy enough to be critical and deplore such materialism. It is often enough done, but seldom very profitably. A rich, or at least a prosperous society can offer a stable foundation for dignity and refinement of living. It can provide the necessary leisure for the cultivation of the arts. Its fruits need not all be purely material: that is obvious enough. It is also, alas, obvious that it can lead to a disastrous fatty degeneration of the soul, and a loss of interest in anything beyond what can be eaten or drunk or lusted after, as every 'affluent society' has eventually found to its cost. The drive of the human race is not to the perfecting of a sleek animal, but to the growth of a soul. Until now, when we have been meditating on the unicorn, the emphasis has been almost entirely on the nature and mystery of *his* activity, on how he comes to us drawn and held captive by his love. Little has been said about the human response. Yet it is significant enough. The growth of a soul is in every way more urgent, because it is more fundamental, than the pursuit of material security. It is towards the unseen, transcendent reality, the source of beauty, the ground of all goodness, that the supreme thrust

33

of all human striving should be aimed. To put it in a sentence, we should remember that man is created for fellowship with God. It is in such fellowship that all his glories lie, and from it that they come, so that apart from such fellowship life must inevitably remain stunted and its potentialities unrealized.

There need be no fear that such a quest will be fruitless or issue only in surfeit and eventually pall, to borrow the phrase of Henri IV, like a diet of *toujours perdrix*. They that hunger and thirst after righteousness shall be filled, said Christ (Matt. 5: 6). That is true certainly, but it is a hunger that will never be satisfied. The more we have, the more we shall want, and the more we shall enjoy. We need in our hearts today a more divine discontent, for the world is so made, and our souls and bodies are so made, that they can sustain love and spirituality to a degree far beyond anything that we have as yet attained. As Paul says, quoting Isaiah, 'Eye hath not seen, nor ear heard, neither have entered into the heart of man, the things which God hath prepared for them that love him. (I Cor. 2: 9). By the indwelling energy of the Spirit of God there is no limit to what we may become.

The hunt is up. But who is the hunter and who is the quarry? Is it man who hunts the unicorn or the unicorn that hunts man? In a strange way it is both, Francis Thompson knew well that Christ had hunted him down with unwearying patience until at last he could run from him no longer. This is the basic truth, as all the saints confess, for if God did not come to us, there is no way conceivable or inconceivable in which we might come to God. But the other is also true. We must seek the Lord while he may be found. We must hunt the unicorn with all the strength we have. We can of course never catch up with him: always he is ahead of us, but as we pursue he draws us ever further on into new, strange country, and in the very pursuit we find a growing intimacy with him that is the secret and the source of all spiritual development, which can increase without limit until the dawning of the perfect day.

34

FEAST OF SAINT STEPHEN:
THE FIRST MARTYR

But my horn shalt thou exalt like the horn of an unicorn:
I shall be anointed with fresh oil. (Ps. 92: 10)

WE learn from the Talmud that this psalm, which is entitled 'A Psalm for the Sabbath Day', was sung during the sacrifice in the Temple of the first lamb of the Sabbath offering. Whatever the reasons may have been that first selected it for this purpose, it is certainly, as Dr Kirkpatrick says, 'a noble conception of the "day of the soul's rest" as a day of joyous thanksgiving and devout meditation on the works of God.'[23] It praises his loving-kindness in the morning and his faithfulness every night; for God has made us glad through his work and we will triumph in the works of his hands.

This brings me directly to the tapestries of the Lady and the Unicorn which were the catalyst of my meditations on the mystery of the unicorn in Christian symbolism. At the Musée de Cluny are six tapestries, similar in design and colouring. Each shows a lady, not always the same lady, standing on an island sparkling with flowers of every colour, and supported on either hand by a lion and an unicorn which hold aloft banners with a coat of arms. Whose arms they are was for long a matter of discussion, and for our purposes it is quite irrelevant. In the case of five of the tapestries the meaning is quite clear. They represent the riches that come to us through the five senses. The first portrays the wealth that is ours through sight, and while the lion is very busy holding his banner erect, the unicorn (having apparently lost his banner somewhere) is gazing, with his front hoofs on the lady's lap, at his own reflection in a mirror that she holds in her right hand. I sense here a reference to the Creator contemplating the works of his hands, and seeing there a faint reflection of his own perfection and beauty. At all events, here in the gifts of sight are revealed to us the richness and wonder of God's creation. The delicate glory of sunrise; the royal grandeur of great sunsets with the sky flaming in gold and crimson; the beauty of the flowers that are all around us in the summer days; the beauty of the human face.

35

In the second tapestry, the lady is seen playing on a portable organ, while both the lion and the unicorn lean on their standards and listen rapturously. Here are all the richness and wonder that come to us through the sense of hearing. It is sometimes discussed by those who have nothing better to do, whether, if we had to choose, we should rather be blind or deaf. Which is the worse affliction? It is a pointless question, for the loss of either sense is an incalculable deprivation. Popular sentiment tends to assume that it is worse to be blind than to be deaf, for the blind can count on unlimited help and sympathy, while the deaf seem only to stir up irritation. It is well said in the Book of Leviticus that not only are we not to put a stumbling block before the blind, but we are not to curse the deaf (Lev. 19: 14). Do not regard them as a nuisance. For indeed the loneliness of the deaf, shut out from all normal conversation, and therefore from all normal communication with other people, is a grievous loss. There can often be a look of sheer desolate aloneness in the eyes of a totally deaf person who finds himself in general company. Be that as it may, how much apart from human companionship the deaf must miss—the glory of great music that can bewilder the soul; the sound of running water in a mountain stream; the song of the birds at dawn, and so much more. Through these two senses of sight and hearing we have access to a wonder and infinite variety that are past computation.

The next three tapestries represent the senses of taste and smell and touch. In the first the lady is feeding titbits to a small bird, while the lion looks on with his tongue hanging out. The unicorn meanwhile pretends not to be interested. In the next she is weaving a garland of flowers, while in the background a monkey somewhat soulfully sniffs at a carnation. In a third, the lady herself holds the lion's standard in her right hand, while with the left she strokes the horn of the unicorn. (But why the deadly horn?) All five taken together represent the fullness of human participation in God's creation, which he has made to be very good, and in which he has allowed man to share. The variety of the riches that floods in upon us through our senses is stupendous, and it is surely only because this has been part and parcel of life from our earliest days that we accept it so calmly. Truly, as the ninety-second psalm says, God has made us glad through his work and we will triumph in the works of his hands.

If there were only these five tapestries, their significance would be simple. They would be a symphonic poem, glorying in the wonder and beauty of the world around us. It is the sixth and last tapestry that is the puzzle. For one thing, it is the only tapestry that has an inscription, which reads quite simply, *'A Mon Seul Désir'*—'To that which has stolen my heart away' (cf. p. vi). But what is the lady doing, and what does the picture mean, and how does it connect with the others? For long enough it was assumed that from a casket of jewels that her attendant is offering her the lady was choosing the richest and the most beautiful necklace that it contained. Does this mean that, having contemplated everything of beauty that her senses show her, she decided that the thing which has won her heart is this necklace? And is the end message of all this pageant of beauty merely the sordid thought that 'diamonds are a girl's best friend'?

Recently a scholar hit on what is undoubtedly the true explanation.[24] The lady is not choosing anything at all out of the casket. On the contrary she is stripping herself of all her jewels, starting with the most valuable, and is heaping them into the casket. The meaning is then clear, however startling. All the rich treasure that she has received through her senses, by sight and hearing, by taste, smell and touch, she is offering back *'A Mon Seul Désir'*. She is stripping herself of everything that has made life full and given it wonder and beauty, and is offering it all back to him who has stolen her heart away. Surely, some will say, this is the sheerest folly.

For there is an idea abroad in these times that the fullness of life depends ultimately on the number of things that we possess and can enjoy. To have lived a full life you must have been everywhere and seen all that there is to be seen, experienced everything that can be experienced, met all kinds of interesting people, and done all sort of unusual and exciting things. But is that the last word in wisdom? St Teresa of Avila sets out in *The Way of Perfection* to teach her nuns how to pray by meditating on the Lord's Prayer. Being, however, an extremely garrulous writer, she is more than half way through the book before she comes within sight of the Our Father, for there are certain things which seem to her to be of the utmost importance for Christians to learn before they can pray successfully. The first is poverty. Then she treats of the fundamental necessity of love—love to God and love to our neighbour. Then, warning us that love is not the surge of emotion that most people imagine it to be, she writes at length of detachment— detachment from all created things, and even from people, in order that we may centre life more firmly in God. Lastly, she writes of humility, which is the fruit of the other three, and without which no one can draw near to God.

It is with detachment that we are concerned here. Teresa teaches that we are to care nothing for any created thing, but embrace the Creator alone This may seem odd advice to a generation that is unendingly proclaiming

37

the need for our being involved with people and with the affairs of the world. It is indeed denounced as a flat repudiation of the Incarnation. Did God, we are asked with a show of indignation, practise detachment from the world when he took our human frame and was made man? I am not so sure that he does not practise detachment: it would otherwise be difficult to understand how men could intelligently deny his existence. He is, as the prophet said, a God who hides himself, and to hide yourself implies at least some degree of detachment. The question before us, however, is the justification for the Christian being detached from the world. It is only justifiable if it is firmly set in the context of love: love to God and love to our neighbour. But it is only God who must be loved without reservation. The point is made with admirable lucidity by St Thérèse of Lisieux when writing to Pauline who was both her own sister and the Mother,

> The longing [i.e. to see you and talk with you] was so strong that I was forced to hurry past your cell and to clutch the balustrade to prevent myself from turning back . . . How glad I am now that I crushed those impulses right from the start of my religious life . . . No longer do I feel that I must refuse to let my heart have any comfort, for my heart is centred on God . . . Because it has loved only Him it has gradually developed until it can manifest to those dear to Him a tenderness incomparably deeper than if it had spent itself in barren selfish love.[25]

Love of all created things, even of our neighbour and of ourself, must have in it a certain detachment or it will be neither pure nor effective. Nothing destroys more quickly or more certainly the good that we can do our neighbour than an excess of emotional feeling or emotional attachment that hinders us again and again from seeing his real need or from being able to give him the support he needs. The surgeon who allowed himself to become emotionally involved in the suffering of his patient would be less efficient than if he were to keep himself somewhat detached. The nurse has to learn not to allow her heart to be torn apart by the sufferings of her patient, or she will fail to give that courage and strength which are essential. The teacher who allows affection to sway his judgement will be considered 'soft', and will certainly not draw the best out of his pupils. The parents who love their children because they are their own—their own flesh and blood, love in the wrong way and become incapable of seeing them as they really are. They will then either seek to dominate them and make them like themselves, or be so indulgent that they allow them to grow up selfish and self-willed.

For such thoughts to be Christian and not simply worldly common-sense, far less some form of Stoic 'apathy', they must be set firmly within the context of the love of God. All detachment from our neighbour which is not rooted in an all-demanding love of God will be cold and heartless and inhuman, for those who love their neighbour most selflessly are those who love God with an utterly selfless love. Then, as St Thérèse says, they will love those dear to God with 'a tenderness incomparably deeper than if it had spent itself in barren selfish love'. For the greatest necessity of all is detachment from self. Without this, I may give all my goods to feed the poor and it will all be worthless. With all the great spiritual directors St Teresa insists on the absolute necessity of detachment from ourself. There is no use, she writes, locking your house up most carefully and even fitting the most perfect of burglar devices, if you lock the burglar inside the house. There is no worse thief than the one who lives in the house, and there is nothing that will steal us away from our whole-hearted devotion to God more dangerously than our own self-will and our attachment to our own self and our own interest. [26]

There is nothing that will separate us from God more ruthlessly than that secret and subtle love of self that haunts us all: the acting to win the approval of the world, that we may be respected and admired: the naive self-approval that knows its own worth even if no one else does. Perhaps the most revolutionary part of the teaching of St Augustine is his insistence that even our good works, our fine actions, our kindly thoughts and our highest and purest aspirations must be surrendered to God. They are God's, and not ours. We must strip ourselves of everything, if we truly love God and seek communion with him. We cannot have the glory of the Sons of God until we become oblivious to our glory, and oblivious to self. There is in Paul's second letter to the Corinthians a passage difficult to translate for many reasons, one of which is that it contains a verb of which we do not know the meaning. But translating it as the Authorized Version does (and there is still a strong case that can be made for this, though modern translators mostly translate differently) Paul speaks of our beholding in a mirror the glory of the Lord (II Cor. 3: 18). This is an odd mirror certainly, for it is the normal function of a looking-glass, when we gaze into it, to reflect our own features. Yet though it may be an awkward enough illustration, it catches the spiritual truth exactly. He who is filled with the love of God and dead to himself sees, wherever he looks, not himself but Christ. The world does not reflect back to him his own features, his needs and desires, his hopes and fears for himself, but it reflects Christ. All things reflect Christ and reflect his glory. Thus we press on towards the goal, *à notre seul*

39

désir, which, so far as we are concerned, is not our own perfecting, but the glory of God and of his Christ.

We do not seek deliberately and consciously to perfect ourselves in any of the Christian virtues. That way lies the deadly sin of self-righteousness. We practise the life of obedience, service and love to God, oblivious to self and self-interest even of the most refined spiritual nature. Fullness of life consists not in the richness of the things we enjoy—even though these things may be friends and companions. It consists, quite certainly, in the richness of the service that we offer to God and in God to our fellow beings, and this without regard to any answering affection that we may find. Does Job serve God for nought: asked sneering Satan,[27] but of course all the saints and holy ones have served God for just that:

> *Not for the sake of winning heaven,*
> *Or of escaping hell;*
> *Not with the hope of gaining aught,*
> *Nor seeking a reward.*[28]

Those whose motives are moulded by a desire to be loved, or even to be popular, rather than by what they know to be right, are doomed to disappointment. After all, our Saviour has warned us that anyone who loves father and mother more than himself is not worthy of him (Matt. 10: 37), which is only to emphasize the fact that God must come first and must come last, and that loyalty to the righteousness of God must never be compromised by affection for any created thing.

That is why the lady in the tapestry quite clearly claims no right to possess as her own any of the rich gifts she has been contemplating. They are God's, and only as belonging to him and for his glory will she use them. She surrenders all and gains all. It is not pretty, poetical language, but a basic principle of all Christian living, when the hymn writer sings,

> *Better than life itself Thy love,*
> *Dearer than all beside to me;*
> *For whom have I in heaven above,*
> *Or what on earth, compared with Thee.*[29]

In her famous illustration from the game of chess, St Teresa speaks of the way in which our soul can put the King of Heaven in check, so that he cannot move out of our power, and indeed will not desire to do so. (Is he not the unicorn who is held captive by love—by his own love?) But, she adds, 'This king does not allow himself to be taken except by one who surrenders wholly to him.'[30] We do not perhaps ponder as deeply as we should the fact that the day after Christmas Day is the Feast of St Stephen, the first martyr—the first who surrendered everything he had, including life, to God, not for any reward that it might bring him, not that he could buy citizenship of the Kingdom of Heaven by giving his all, but simply because he loved God. God came first and last, and all other things must be sacrificed *à son seul désir.* To what purpose was this waste? the disciples asked indignantly when the woman poured the precious flask of ointment on the head of our Lord (cf. Matt. 26: 6—13). But she did not think it waste, and none who have sacrificed everything for the love of Christ have ever thought it waste. It is given to the one supreme love of their life, and here life reaches its culmination.

The foundation on which all spiritual life is built is still: *whosoever will save his life shall lose it: and whosoever will lose his life for Christ's sake shall find it.* For it is gloriously true that those who abandon themselves completely to God, seeking nothing for themselves and claiming nothing as their own, find in the triumphant words of Paul (cf. I Cor. 3: 21—23) that all things are theirs: the world, or life, or death, or things present, or things to come: all are theirs; and they are Christ's; and Christ is God's.

NOTES

1. Oliver Goldsmith, *The Deserted Village*.
2. Arthur H. Curtis, *The Vision and Mission of Jesus*, p. xvi.
3. Søren Kierkegaard, *Training in Christianity* (Quoted from Charles Williams, *The New Christian Year*).
4. Richard Jefferies, *Bevis: The Story of a Boy*.
5. St Teresa of Avila, *The Interior Castle*, Fourth Mansion, Ch. 1.
6. Shakespeare, *Macbeth*, V. v. 23.
7. Isaac Watts, 'Blest morning, whose first dawning rays'.
8. Dietrich Bonhoeffer, *Letters and Papers from Prison*, Ed. Bethge, pp. 360–61.
9. Paul Tillich, *Systematic Theology*, Vol. I, p. 278.
10. Edward Henry Bickersteth, 'Peace, perfect peace, in this dark world of sin'.
11. Lightfoot, *Commentary on Philippians*, Ch. 3, v. 10.
12. Shakespeare, *Lucrece*, 956.
13. Lord Acton (Quoted in *The Life and Letters of Mandell Creighton*).
14. G.K. Chesterton, *Ballad of the White Horse*.
15. Karl Barth, *Church Dogmatics*, III, X, 47, p. 454.
16. Calvin, *Commentary on Mark, in loco*.
17. Henry Drummond, Address on 'The Eccentricity of Religion'.
18. W.H. Auden, *New Year Letter*.
19. F.H. Bradley, *Ethical Studies* (Footnote to Essay VI).
20. Robert Bridges, *Testament of Beauty*, I.781.
21. 15th century hymn, *Caelestis formam gloriae*, Trans. J.M. Neale.
22. Adamnan, *Life of St Columba*, III. 23. 4.
23. A.F. Kirkpatrick, *Commentary on Psalms, in loco*.
24. Alain Erlande-Brandenburg, *La Dame à Licorne*.
25. St Thérèse of Lisieux, *Autobiography*, Ch. 36.
26. St Teresa of Avila, *The Way of Perfection*, Ch. X.
27. Job 1: 9 (The actual word in the AV is 'fear' and not 'serve').
28. Seventeenth century hymn, *O Deus ego amo te*, Trans. Edward Caswall.
29. James Montgomery, 'O God, thou art my God alone'.
30. St Teresa of Avila, *The Way of Perfection*, Ch. XVI.